Pelkola, Elsa
Indiana

## CORE LIBRARY OF US STATES

# INDIANA

**BY ELSA PELKOLA**

**CONTENT CONSULTANT**
Bethany Hrachovec, MA
Director of Education and Engagement
Indiana Historical Society

abdobooks.com

Published by Abdo Publishing, a division of ABDO, PO Box 398166, Minneapolis, Minnesota 55439. Copyright © 2023 by Abdo Consulting Group, Inc. International copyrights reserved in all countries. No part of this book may be reproduced in any form without written permission from the publisher. Core Library™ is a trademark and logo of Abdo Publishing.

Printed in the United States of America, North Mankato, Minnesota.
052022
092022

Cover Photo: Shutterstock Images
Interior Photos: Grindstone Media Group/Shutterstock Images, 4–5, 45; Red Line Editorial, 7 (Indiana), 7 (USA); Nagel Photography/Shutterstock Images, 9; N1808/Glenn A. Black Laboratory of Archaeology/Indiana University Museum of Archaeology and Anthropology and the Trustees of Indiana University, 12–13; Shutterstock Images, 17 (flag); Ernie Decker/iStockphoto, 17 (bird); iStockphoto, 17 (flower); Brandon Alms/Shutterstock Images, 17 (firefly); Peter Turner Photography/Shutterstock Images, 17 (tree); North Wind Picture Archives/AP Images, 18; Rudy Balasko/iStockphoto, 21; Delmas Lehman/Shutterstock Images, 22–23, 43; Bettmann/Getty Images, 25; MerlinTuttle.org/Science Source, 26; Aaron Yoder/iStockphoto, 30–31; Sean Pavone/Shutterstock Images, 34; Denis Makarenko/Shutterstock Images, 36–37; Jeffrey M. Frank/Shutterstock Images, 38

Editor: Angela Lim
Series Designer: Joshua Olson

**Library of Congress Control Number: 2021951394**

**Publisher's Cataloging-in-Publication Data**

Names: Pelkola, Elsa, author.
Title: Indiana / by Elsa Pelkola
Description: Minneapolis, Minnesota : Abdo Publishing, 2023 | Series: Core library of US states | Includes online resources and index.
Identifiers: ISBN 9781532197550 (lib. bdg.) | ISBN 9781098270315 (ebook)
Subjects: LCSH: U.S. states--Juvenile literature. | Midwest States--Juvenile literature. | Indiana--History--Juvenile literature. | Physical geography--United States--Juvenile literature.
Classification: DDC 977.2--dc23

Population demographics broken down by race and ethnicity come from the 2019 census estimate. Population totals come from the 2020 census.

# CONTENTS

**CHAPTER ONE**
**The Hoosier State** .................. 4

**CHAPTER TWO**
**History of Indiana** ................. 12

**CHAPTER THREE**
**Geography and Climate** .......... 22

**CHAPTER FOUR**
**Resources and Economy** .......... 30

**CHAPTER FIVE**
**People and Places** ................. 36

Important Dates ....................... 42

Stop and Think ........................ 44

Glossary ................................ 46

Online Resources ..................... 47

Learn More ............................ 47

Index ................................... 48

About the Author ..................... 48

CHAPTER ONE

# THE HOOSIER STATE

**B**rightly colored race cars roar down the track. It is Memorial Day weekend. Heat rises from the blacktop as the sound of engines fills the air. Hundreds of cheering people are packed in the grandstands at the Indianapolis Motor Speedway. It is the largest sporting venue by seating in the world. The crowd's excitement rises as the cars race each other for 500 miles (805 km). The people are watching the Indianapolis (Indy) 500, one of the most famous racing events in the world.

The Indianapolis Motor Speedway grandstands can seat approximately 250,000 people.

The first Indy 500 took place in 1911. Indiana has hosted the thrilling event ever since.

No one knows how Indiana's nickname came to be. But people from the Hoosier State are proud of it. Today it represents strong, friendly, and hardworking people.

## ABOUT INDIANA

Indiana is part of the Midwest. This region of the United States is located in the middle of the country. Indiana is bordered by four states. Ohio lies to the east. The Ohio River forms the state's southern border.

### WHAT'S A HOOSIER?

There are a few theories about where the nickname Hoosiers came from. Many think the name came from poet John Finley's work, "The Hoosier's Nest." Others trace the nickname back to a contractor named Hoosier. He hired employees from Indiana to work on the Louisville and Portland Canal. They became known as "Hoosier's Men." No matter where the nickname originated, it is widely accepted that Hoosiers have a friendly attitude and care about their neighbors.

# MAP OF INDIANA

Indiana has many large cities and major waterways. How does this map help you understand what the state has to offer?

7

Kentucky lies on the other side of the river. Illinois is to the west of Indiana. Michigan and Lake Michigan make Indiana's northern border.

Like other Midwest states, Indiana is known for agriculture and manufacturing. Indiana is also part of the Corn Belt. This group of states produces a lot of corn and other crops.

Indianapolis is the largest city in the state. It is also the state's capital. The Soldiers and Sailors Monument is located in downtown Indianapolis. It honors Hoosiers who fought in some of the nation's wars, such as the American Civil War (1861–1865). Several major highways cross through Indianapolis. This is one reason the state's motto is "Crossroads of America." In the 1920s the state's highways helped connect eastern states to western regions. People passed through the state to move out West.

Indiana has other cities as well. Fort Wayne is located in the northeast. Fitting to Indiana's motto,

The University of Notre Dame's golden dome is covered in 23.9 karat gold leaf. These gold flakes are also used to paint the helmets of the school's football team.

Fort Wayne is within a day's drive of other major cities in the region. These include large Midwest cities such as Chicago, Illinois, and Cleveland, Ohio. People enjoy shopping and going to farmers markets in downtown Bloomington. South Bend, Indiana, is home to the University of Notre Dame. Fans of Notre Dame football gather at the campus on game day weekends and take pictures in front of the iconic Golden Dome.

## PERSPECTIVES

### WHY LOVE INDIANA?

Many people move to Indiana because they want to work and live in small cities. Indianapolis and South Bend are not as crowded as New York or Los Angeles. But they still offer vibrant city life. Other reasons some people love Indiana include the community. Journalist Tim Swarens said, "Over the 20 years that I've called Indiana home, I have met people who care deeply about their neighbors and their communities." Indiana offers a lower cost of living, easy access to many types of parks and recreation, and a small-town feel.

Indiana may be the Crossroads of America, but it is more than just a state to pass through. Big cities have many attractions. Sports fans enjoy events such as the Indy 500 and Notre Dame football. The state also has beautiful natural landscapes. There is something for everyone in the Hoosier State.

# STRAIGHT TO THE SOURCE

In 1977 Janet Guthrie became the first woman to compete in the Indy 500. She spoke about breaking into a male-dominated sport:

*The general idea was women don't have the strength, the endurance, the emotional stability. . . . The only way to deal with that was on the racetrack. There was no other way to do it. The guys just had to get the experience of driving against me and then, as I say, things changed. . . If the guys were saying this driver is a female and therefore, she is no good, and then the no-good driver blows your doors off, you have to change your position a little.*

Source: Heidi Glenn and Victoria Whitley-Berry. "Indy 500 Pioneer Janet Guthrie Savors the Day She Made History." *NPR*, 27 May 2018, npr.org. Accessed 25 May 2021.

## BACK IT UP

The author of this passage is using evidence to support a point. Write a paragraph describing the point the author is making. Then write down two or three pieces of evidence the author uses to make the point.

# CHAPTER TWO

# HISTORY OF INDIANA

People have lived in Indiana since 10,000 BCE. Early cultures include the Hopewell tradition, which appeared approximately 2,000 years ago. These peoples built burial mounds around 250 BCE that can still be seen today. Cultures began to rely more on agriculture beginning around 1000 CE. Historians are still studying the connection of these cultures to American Indian nations today, many of which were established

Indiana archaeologist Glenn Black studied sites such as the Angel Mounds State Historic Site in the 1950s. Archaeologists study early cultures.

by the 1600s. These include the Shawnee, Miami, and Potawatomi.

## WARS AND CONFLICTS

In the 1600s a large chunk of North America belonged to the French, including what is now Indiana. Both British colonists and French traders were in the Indiana region at this time. They traded with American Indian nations. The British and the French both wanted total control of this trade. They threatened the American Indians. Both European groups would respond with

### FRENCH EXPLORATION

René-Robert Cavelier de La Salle was a French explorer. He was one of the first Europeans to enter the Indiana region. In 1679 he sailed south from French territory in Canada. La Salle traveled across Lake Michigan and continued down the Saint Joseph River. He hoped to establish trading forts there. He and his crew set up camp for the winter along a southern bend in the river. This location would later become South Bend.

violence if American Indian peoples were found trading with their rival.

Tensions between the British and the French colonists eventually led to the French and Indian War (1754–1763). American Indians fought on both sides. The British were victorious, forcing the French to give up much of their land, including Canada and everything east of the Mississippi River. Present-day Indiana was a part of this land.

British colonists wanted to expand into this new land. But the British government would not allow it. The region west of the Appalachian Mountains still belonged to the American Indian nations, a policy that won Great Britain favor with the American Indian peoples. The policy stayed in place until after the Revolutionary War (1775–1783). This is when the United States won freedom from Great Britain.

In 1780 the US Congress opened the lands west of the Appalachian Mountains for settlement. This region was called the Northwest Territory. It was divided into two parts in 1800, forming the Indiana Territory. At its largest, this territory included land that would become Indiana, Illinois, Wisconsin, Michigan, and part of Minnesota. The land was split into even smaller territories over time.

The United States was at war again with Great Britain in 1812. Tensions between American Indians and US settlers were also high. US settlers continued to move into American Indian land. Because of this, many American Indians sided with the British during the war. A Shawnee leader named Tecumseh worked with many other American Indian peoples. He believed that together the nations would be able to stop US expansion westward. American Indian nations and the US Army clashed at the Battle of Tippecanoe in 1811. Some historians consider this battle to be the start of the War of 1812 (1812–1815). Tecumseh was killed in battle in 1813. American Indian nations had

# INDIANA
# QUICK FACTS

State symbols represent the state. How do these facts and symbols help you understand Indiana's history and geography?

**Abbreviation:** IN
**Nickname:** The Hoosier State
**Motto:** Crossroads of America
**Date of statehood:** December 11, 1816
**Capital:** Indianapolis
**Population:** 6,785,528
**Area:** 36,420 square miles (94,327 sq km)

## STATE SYMBOLS

**State bird**
Northern cardinal

**State insect**
Say's firefly

**State flower**
Peony

**State tree**
Tulip poplar

Tecumseh and other American Indian people sided with the British during the War of 1812.

experienced heavy losses. Many stopped fighting after the death of their leader.

Ultimately the United States defeated Great Britain. US settlers continued to push westward. Many of the American Indian nations living in Indiana moved out of the region. Some nations, such as the Shawnee, had no choice but to leave because of the growing number of US settlers. The Miami were forced to leave by the US government.

Indiana became the nineteenth US state on December 11, 1816. It entered as a free state, meaning slavery was illegal. However, those who were enslaved before statehood were not set free after Indiana became a state. The issue of slavery led to the Civil War (1861–1865). Indiana joined the Union, a group of northern states fighting against slavery. Nearly 200,000 Hoosiers served in the Civil War. The Union was victorious in 1865, and slavery was banned throughout the United States.

## PERSPECTIVES
### THE UNDERGROUND RAILROAD

The Underground Railroad was not a real railroad. It was a network of routes that connected slave states to free states in the North. People along the Underground Railroad would help enslaved people escape by hiding them in their homes. This was illegal.

The Levi and Catherine Coffin House in Indiana was a stop on the Underground Railroad. The Coffin family hid and helped more than 1,000 formerly enslaved people. Levi Coffin said, "I . . . did not feel bound to respect human laws that came in direct [conflict] with the law of God."

## INDIANA IN THE 1900s

In the 1900s Indiana saw a growth of cities and industries. The United States Steel Corporation built a new steel mill in the state around the turn of the century. Steel could be used to make automobiles. Indiana became an important part of the automobile industry.

These steel mills were important during World War II (1939–1945). They helped produce wartime materials. One steel town grew from a population of 890 people to 15,000 during the war. In addition more than 450,000 Hoosiers served in the war.

## GOVERNMENT

Indiana has three branches of government. The legislative branch is made up of the Senate and the House of Representatives. This branch votes on laws. The governor is the head of the executive branch. Governors sign new laws to make them official. The judicial branch consists of the state's courts,

The capitol building in Indianapolis stands approximately 235 feet (72 m) tall.

including the Indiana Supreme Court. This branch reviews laws.

The Pokagon Band of Potawatomi Indians is the only federally recognized tribe in Indiana. The nation has a separate government system. Many other American Indian nations have connections to Indiana that go back hundreds of years.

CHAPTER
THREE

# GEOGRAPHY AND CLIMATE

Indiana's geography is mainly open and flat. The northern region of the state is dotted with lakes. Indiana's northern shoreline with Lake Michigan became a national park in 2019. Visitors can see rolling sand dunes. A dune is a mound or hill made of sand. Wind and water form dunes that can sometimes reach 200 feet (60 m). Visitors can camp, fish, or hike at Indiana Dunes National Park.

Flat plains dominate the central part of the state. Approximately 17,000 years ago,

**Visitors to the Indiana Dunes National Park can enjoy scenic views of Lake Michigan.**

glaciers covered this region. As these glaciers moved slowly across Indiana, they left behind fertile soils. Today farmers depend on these soils to produce crops.

Southern Indiana is the hilliest region of the state. This is because glaciers did not reach this region. Hoosier Hill is Indiana's highest point in elevation. It is located in south-central Indiana. It stands at 1,257 feet (383 m).

Temperatures change greatly between Indiana's seasons. In the summer, temperatures can climb past 100 degrees Fahrenheit (38°C). The low temperature averages 15 degrees Fahrenheit (−9°C) in the winter.

Precipitation varies throughout the state. Indiana receives an average of 42 inches (107 cm) of rainfall each year. The land area near Lake Michigan experiences heavy snow. This is because of the lake effect, caused by cold air passing over Lake Michigan. The water in the lake is warmer than the air temperature. This temperature difference causes

Indiana residents made a wall of sandbags to hold back floodwater near Fort Wayne in 1982.

moisture to rise, leading to large amounts of snowfall. Snowfall averages 76 inches (193 cm) a year near Lake Michigan. An average of just 14 inches (36 cm) falls in the southwestern part of the state.

Indiana does not experience tornadoes as often as other states in the Midwest. But the state is still at

The Indiana bat is an endangered species. It hunts insects at night.

risk for these extreme weather events. A major tornado touched down in Indiana in 2012. And the deadliest tornado in US history ripped through Indiana and two other states in 1925. The Tri-State Tornado killed 695 people.

## PLANTS AND ANIMALS

More than 20 percent of Indiana is forested. These forests are home to many types of animals. Black bears, white-tailed deer, and squirrels are just a few of Indiana's forest mammals. The northern cardinal is Indiana's state bird. It can be found in forests and neighborhoods.

The majority of the state's forests consist of hardwood trees such as oak and hickory. The tulip poplar tree is Indiana's state tree. Despite its name, it is not a poplar tree. It is a type of magnolia that grows beautiful, greenish-yellow flowers that are shaped like tulips. Peonies are large flowers that come in different colors, such as red, pink, or yellow. They bloom in late May and early June. The peony has been the state's flower since 1957.

## PERSPECTIVES
### SAY'S FIREFLY

In 2014 Indiana was one of just three states that did not have a state insect. A group of second graders led efforts to name an official state insect. They wrote letters to Indiana government officials. Say's firefly became the official state insect in 2018.

Governor Eric Holcomb made it official. He spoke of the students' dedication. "Beyond the satisfaction these kids will feel when they look out on a hot Indiana summer night and see the state insect flashing away, the real beauty of this bill is the [political] engagement it inspired in our youngest citizens."

The Wabash River is one of the longest rivers in Indiana. It runs for approximately 475 miles (764 km) through the state. It eventually flows into the Ohio River. The river is home to 150 types of fish. Some of these are endangered. This includes the paddlefish, one of the oldest-known types of fish in the world. Fossil records date these fish back to around the time of dinosaurs.

## LAKE STURGEON

The lake sturgeon is an endangered fish in Indiana. An adult often weighs up to 45 pounds (20 kg). Lake sturgeons were once found in many Indiana lakes and waterways. But a dam on the East Fork White River blocks breeding grounds for the fish. In Indiana the lake sturgeon can be found in only 50 miles (80 km) of this river, which flows through southern Indiana. Some people are trying to get the state to remove the dam.

# STRAIGHT TO THE SOURCE

The Tri-State Tornado was the deadliest tornado in US history. Lela Hartman was a young girl visiting family on an Indiana farm in 1925 when it hit. In 2013 she described her memory of the event:

*We didn't have—you were your weather forecaster. You watched the sky. Well, it was . . . such a pretty day that day. . . . And for March, that was a little bit unusual in itself. But then, after noon, when it began to turn dark and. . . . You know, I can't remember that it lightninged and thundered, but it's bound to have. All I remember is how dark it kept gettin', and the wind, you know? . . . I was scared. I wanted to go to the cellar. But there wasn't a one of us would go until Grandma would go. And she wasn't about to go. But she . . . finally did. I think she finally decided that something was about to give.*

Source: Marc Herman. "A Survivor of the Deadliest Tornado in US History Tells Her Tale." *Pacific Standard*, 14 June 2017, psmag.com. Accessed 19 May 2021.

## WHAT'S THE BIG IDEA?

Take a close look at this passage. What is the main connection that the speaker makes between weather predictions in 1925 and weather predictions today? How does modern technology help us prepare better for storms?

# CHAPTER FOUR

# RESOURCES AND ECONOMY

As a Corn Belt state, agriculture is one of Indiana's major industries. The state is a top producer of corn, soybeans, and mint in the United States. Tomatoes and watermelons are major fruits grown there. Indiana is also a leading producer of hogs, dairy, and poultry such as turkeys.

But agriculture is not the only major industry in the state. Workers mine stone for building and coal. Indiana limestone has helped build many famous structures in the

**Agriculture brings in approximately $31.2 billion to Indiana each year.**

## POPCORN KING

Orville Redenbacher grew up on a farm in Indiana. He started work on a new type of popcorn at age 12. He loved his work so much that he went to Purdue University in West Lafayette. There he got a degree in agriculture. His lighter and fluffier popcorn became famous. Orville Redenbacher's popcorn remains one of the most popular snacks in the United States today.

United States such as the Empire State Building, the Pentagon, and the Indiana State Capitol. The state produces 36 million tons (33 million metric tons) of coal a year. The timber industry brings in $3 billion annually.

## MANUFACTURING AND HEALTH CARE

Manufacturing is an important part of Indiana's economy. In 2018 Indiana was the top producer of steel in the United States. The state's wood supply helps people make hardwood furniture, caskets, and some musical instruments. The state is also a major exporter of cars and car parts.

Indiana cities are important economic centers. Many national companies are headquartered in Indianapolis. Health care is one major industry for the city. Anthem is one of the nation's largest health insurance companies. Its headquarters are in Indianapolis. Eli Lilly is a pharmaceutical company based in the city. Scientists at Eli Lilly work to develop new medicines that can be used around the world.

## PERSPECTIVES

### THRIVING CAR INDUSTRY

Indiana once led the way with gas-powered automobiles. In 1919 the state had 172 companies that built cars or car parts. These companies were spread across more than 30 cities and towns. This was known as the Automotive Belt. The belt included cities such as Gary, South Bend, Fort Wayne, Indianapolis, and many others. The most successful carmakers were the Studebaker Brothers, based in South Bend. Studebaker National Museum curator Drew Van De Wielle said, "Hoosiers loved cars so much because the auto industry put a lot of food on a lot of tables." Today Indiana ranks third in auto manufacturing.

Limestone from Indiana was used to make the Soldiers and Sailors Monument in Indianapolis.

## TOURISM

Tourism plays a major role in Indiana's economy. Approximately 5 percent of Hoosiers work in the tourism industry. This includes jobs related to travel, food services, and entertainment. In 2019 Indiana welcomed 81 million visitors. That year, travelers spent $13.2 billion in the state.

Visitors to Indianapolis enjoy trendy restaurants, art museums, and shopping centers. But the state also has plenty of natural spaces to explore, including 24 state parks. Brown County State Park is Indiana's largest state park. It attracts an average of more than 1 million people each year. People enjoy hiking, camping, and horseback riding in the forested park.

## FURTHER EVIDENCE

Chapter Four discusses Indiana's economy and natural resources. What was one of the main points of this chapter? What evidence is included to support this point? Read the article at the website below. Does the information on the website support the main point of the chapter? Does it present new evidence?

### THE HISTORY MUSEUM
abdocorelibrary.com/indiana

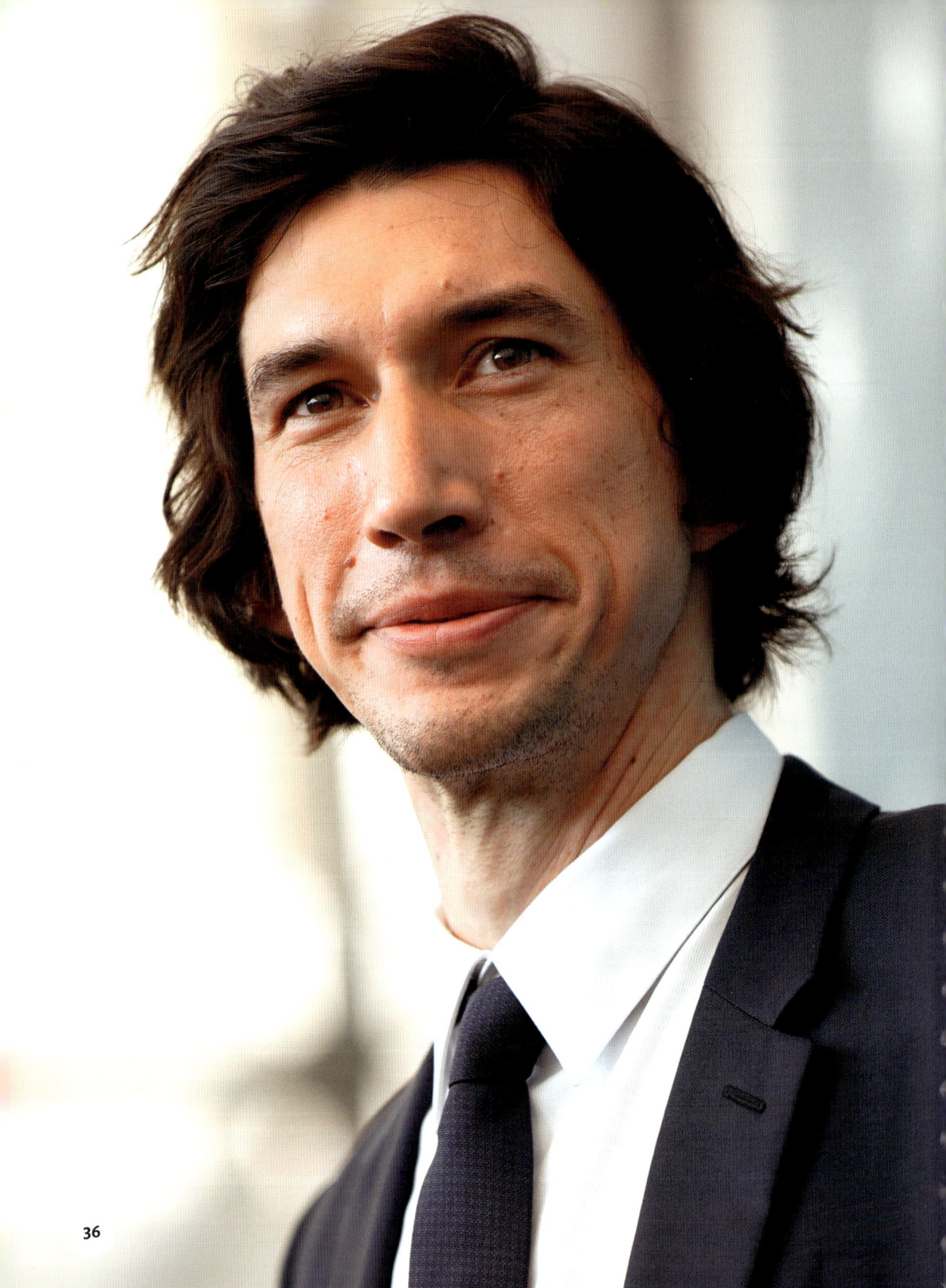

CHAPTER
# FIVE

# PEOPLE AND PLACES

Nearly 7 million people call Indiana home. Approximately 78 percent of Indiana's population is non-Hispanic white. Ten percent of the state's population is Black, and approximately 7 percent is Hispanic or Latino. Another 3 percent is Asian, and less than 1 percent is American Indian.

## IMPORTANT PLACES

Indiana has many natural spaces to explore. One is the Marengo Cave. People have been

Adam Driver, who lived in Indiana for much of his early life, played Kylo Ren in the *Star Wars* sequel trilogy.

**Marengo Cave began forming approximately 1 million years ago.**

exploring the cave since 1883. Parts of the cave system are underwater. Visitors can take guided tours along the Dripstone Trail, which showcases stalagmites and other cave formations.

Indiana is also home to several major colleges. Purdue University has a historic aerospace program.

Neil Armstrong, the first human to walk on the moon, was a Purdue graduate. The University of Notre Dame is ranked as one of the top 25 schools in the nation. Founded in 1820, Indiana University in Bloomington is the largest university in the state.

Indianapolis offers many attractions, like art museums, theaters, and an orchestra hall. The Indianapolis Zoo is a great place for visitors to explore animal exhibits, an

## PERSPECTIVES

### NOTRE DAME FOOTBALL

The University of Notre Dame has one of the best college football programs in the country. The university's football team, the Fighting Irish, has won 11 national titles. The Fighting Irish started playing football in 1887. Since then seven Notre Dame football players have won the Heisman trophy. This award is given to the best college football player each year. Some Notre Dame football players continue on to play professionally. Joe Montana was a quarterback from Notre Dame. He joined the San Francisco 49ers in 1979. He went on to lead the 49ers to four Super Bowls.

## MADAM C. J. WALKER

Born in Louisiana in 1867, Madam C. J. Walker became the first female self-made millionaire in the United States. This meant she did not inherit the wealth through family or marriage. She created hair care products for Black women like herself. Her Indianapolis-based business attracted national attention in 1910. The Madam Walker Legacy Center still stands in Indianapolis today. The building that served as the headquarters for Walker's business is now a historic landmark.

aquarium, and a botanical garden. Families also have fun at the world-famous Children's Museum of Indianapolis. It is the biggest children's museum in the world and offers five floors of interactive exhibits. History museums such as the Indiana Historical Society and Indiana State Museum are also located in the capital city.

Indianapolis has several professional sports teams. The Colts play football in Lucas Oil Stadium. The city is also home to two professional basketball teams. The Pacers are an NBA team, and the Fever are a WNBA team. The National Collegiate Athletic Association Hall of Champions is also located in Indianapolis. This space includes a museum that celebrates college sports and athletes.

Many famous people have come from Indiana, including famous basketball stars Larry Bird and Louie Dampier. Actor Adam Driver grew up in Indiana. From famous people and sports teams to big cities and lakeshores, the Hoosier State has lots to offer. There is plenty to see and experience at the Crossroads of America.

## EXPLORE ONLINE

Chapter Five discusses just a few of the attractions of Indiana. Visit the website below. What other surprising or fun facts about the Hoosier State can you learn about?

### FUN FACTS ABOUT INDIANAPOLIS YOU MIGHT NOT HAVE KNOWN

abdocorelibrary.com/indiana

# IMPORTANT DATES

**10,000 BCE**
The first peoples live in Indiana.

**1600s CE**
Many American Indian nations are established in Indiana, including the Shawnee, Miami, and Potawatomi.

**1800**
The US government creates the Indiana Territory.

**1811**
American Indian nations and the US Army fight at the Battle of Tippecanoe. American Indians continue to be pushed out of the region.

**1816**
Indiana becomes the nineteenth US state on December 11.

**1820**
Indiana University at Bloomington is founded.

**1911**
The first Indianapolis 500 race takes place.

**1925**
The Tri-State Tornado hits Indiana and two other states. It is one of the deadliest tornadoes in US history.

**2018**
Say's firefly becomes the official state insect of Indiana.

**2019**
Indiana's northern shoreline with Lake Michigan becomes a national park.

# STOP AND THINK

### Dig Deeper
After reading this book, what questions do you still have about the animals that live in Indiana? With an adult's help, find a few reliable sources that can help answer these questions. Write a short paragraph about what you learned.

### Why Do I Care?
Maybe you do not live in Indiana. But that doesn't mean you can't think about the important industries Indiana has. What kind of natural resources are found in the state? What types of industries is Indiana known for? How might your life be different without these industries and resources?

### You Are There
This book describes different museums, sports venues, and other places to visit in Indianapolis. Imagine you are taking a trip to Indiana's capital city. Write a letter home telling your friends about your activities in the city. Be sure to add plenty of detail to your notes.

## Another View

This book talks about Tecumseh and the Battle of Tippecanoe. As you know, every source is different. Ask a librarian or another adult to help you find another source about this event. Write a short essay comparing and contrasting the new source's point of view with that of this book's author. What is the point of view of each author? How are they similar and why? How are they different and why?

# GLOSSARY

**aerospace**
a science related to the skies and outer space

**economy**
a place's system of goods, services, money, and jobs

**elevation**
the height above sea level

**endangered**
at risk of dying out

**fertile**
rich in nutrients for growing plants

**glacier**
a large body of ice that moves across land

**illegal**
not allowed by law

**insurance company**
a type of business that financially protects a person's health or belongings

**pharmaceutical**
relating to the production or sale of medicines or drugs

**territory**
an area of land that is not a state but is still controlled by a country

# ONLINE RESOURCES

To learn more about Indiana, visit our free resource websites below.

Visit **abdocorelibrary.com** or scan this QR code for free Common Core resources for teachers and students, including vetted activities, multimedia, and booklinks, for deeper subject comprehension.

Visit **abdobooklinks.com** or scan this QR code for free additional online weblinks for further learning. These links are routinely monitored and updated to provide the most current information available.

# LEARN MORE

Cooper, Robert. *Indianapolis Colts*. Abdo, 2020.

Sjonger, Rebecca. *Tecumseh: Speech at Vincennes*. Crabtree, 2019.

# INDEX

agriculture, 8, 13, 24, 31, 32
American Indians, 13–18, 21
automobiles, 5, 32–33

botanical gardens, 40

Children's Museum of Indianapolis, 40
Corn Belt, 8, 31
Crossroads of America, 8, 10, 17, 41

forests, 26–27, 32, 35
French and Indian War, 15

Indiana University, 39
Indianapolis, 5, 7, 8, 10, 17, 33, 35, 39–41
Indianapolis 500, 5–6, 10, 11

La Salle, René-Robert Cavelier de, 14
Lake Michigan, 7, 8, 14, 23–25
lake sturgeon, 28

manufacturing, 8, 32–33
mining, 31–32

Purdue University, 32, 38–39

Redenbacher, Orville, 32

Say's firefly, 17, 27
South Bend, 7, 9–10, 14, 33

Tecumseh, 16–18
tourism, 34–35, 38
Tri-State Tornado, 26, 29

Underground Railroad, 19
University of Notre Dame, 9–10, 39

Wabash River, 7, 28
Walker, Madam C. J., 40

## About the Author

Elsa Pelkola lives in the Midwest and is an author of many nonfiction books for kids. She also loves popcorn.